yes, we can! He Can HEAL

HEALTH & EDUCATION

QUARRY

yes, we can! He Can HEAL

HEALTH & EDUCATION

Inspiring Stories of Men Who Changed the World

JONATHAN JURAVICH
2023 National Elementary Art Teacher of the Year

RICHARD V. REEVES
Founder of the American Institute for Boys and Men

QUARRY

Quarto.com

This library edition published in 2026 by Quarry Books,
an imprint of The Quarto Group.

100 Cummings Center, Suite 265-D, Beverly, MA 01915, USA.
T (978) 282-9590 F (978) 283-2742

Illustrations by Chris King

Distributed in the United States and Canada
by Lerner Publisher Services
241 First Avenue North
Minneapolis, MN 55401 U.S.A.
www.lernerbooks.com

First Library Edition

Library of Congress Cataloging-in-Publication Control Number: 2025031594

Printed in China

10 9 8 7 6 5 4 3 2 1

For Ari and Josie, who remind me
to seek joy in life's small moments.
—JJ

For Bryce, an inspiring educator
and cherished son.
— RR

Contents

Health

Education

Introduction

My youngest son, Cameron, was about six. I was driving him home after seeing the doctor. We were quiet for a time. Then he said, "Dad, I didn't know men could be doctors."

The doctor we had just seen was a man. But I realized that until that day, every doctor he had ever seen had been a woman. So it was not silly for him to think that being a doctor was something only women did.

But stop to consider this for a moment. That's amazing progress. Women were not even allowed to be doctors for most of human history! For women to be the only doctors in Cameron's world shows how relatively quickly and overwhelmingly stereotypes can be overcome.

I told Cameron then, and I am telling you now, yes, men can be doctors! But just as important, men can be *nurses*, too. Maybe that one sounds strange to you because most nurses are still women. But there are thousands of amazing nurses who are men. It is a great job for a man, and do not let anybody tell you otherwise! There are no rules about what jobs men can do.

This book series is about the sorts of jobs that are sometimes wrongly seen as jobs for women but are just as much for men.

Men like Joe Hogan, who wanted to be a nurse but was told he was not allowed to be. That was because the nearby college teaching nursing only admitted women! In 1982 the Supreme Court said the school had to open its doors to men, and Joe got his wish.

Men like Will Pooley, who was working in Africa to save people's lives from the Ebola virus when he got sick with the disease himself. Once he had recovered, what did Will do? He went back to Africa to carry on his work.

Men like Hector Hugo Gonzalez, who served in the Vietnam War and ended up as president of the National Association of Hispanic Nurses in 1982.

Back during that car ride with Cameron, we talked about teachers. There were no men teaching at his elementary school, so he was not sure men could do that job either. In most countries, fewer men are teaching today than they used to. In the United States, only 23 percent of teachers are men now, compared with 33 percent in 1980.

But men can be teachers! In fact, I think we need men teaching and coaching in our schools more than ever.

Maybe you are more interested in STEM jobs, in which case, great! But maybe not. Maybe you are more interested in working with people, which is great, too. These are what I call "HEAL" subjects and jobs: in health, education, arts, and literacy. Nurses, teachers, childcare workers, therapists, social workers, assistants, psychologists: These are all HEAL jobs.

In recent years, girls have been encouraged to believe that they can be anything they want. That includes jobs that people once thought were "men's jobs." Now there are almost as many women as men working as doctors, lawyers, and scientists. Women fly fighter planes, fight fires, and pass laws. Maybe you even know some of them. This is amazing and wonderful.

But adults have not done as well yet showing that men can also do the things that are still thought of as "women's jobs," mostly in those HEAL professions. Just like girls used to be told that math or science was not right for girls, today boys too often get the message that nursing or social work or teaching are not "manly," or something equally stupid.

So, I am going to be honest with you. Right now it takes some courage to say you are thinking about one of these jobs, say, as a teacher or nurse. One of my other sons, Bryce, is a teacher, working with younger students. As a man, sometimes he has had to work extra hard to pursue this dream. He has not always been encouraged by others. But he is not going to let other people's views stop him. Nor will you, I hope.

Men can be nurses. Men can be teachers. Jermar Rountree from Washington, D.C., was a finalist for National Teacher of the Year and loves his job. He says, "I love what I do, and that will not change. I am dedicated to my kids, families, and colleagues. I want to be that trusted person, that father figure, that coach that my students can rely on no matter what."

Did you know that John Adams, the second president of the United States, was a classroom teacher? So was Archbishop Desmond Tutu, a hero to the people of South Africa for his fight for justice.

These are men who matter, whom you can count on. They offer a helping hand, not a clenched fist. They are brave men doing hard work to make life better for all of us. They are providers of care, love, practical assistance, safety, and learning.

Men can be psychologists or counselors, helping people who are sad or lonely. Men can be social workers, helping families and people who are in trouble. These are men like Warren McAdams, who went from being a volunteer firefighter to making it a career, often helping families with sick children, and men like Josh Bower, a police officer in the K9 unit working with dogs who became a counselor so that he could help people before they got into trouble, rather than afterward.

Lots of the men who choose these jobs, which some people insultingly think are "women's jobs," are proud of their work. Nurse Ben Medina says, "Nursing as a career has been such a blessing. It is a fantastic, amazing profession. Every day I'm excited to go to work."

Teachers, counselors, nurses. These men are heroes, I think, in a different but equal way to firefighters and pilots and soldiers. They know they are making a difference in other people's lives. They are pillars of strength in the lives of people who need them most. Maybe you could be one, too. Why not?

—Richard V. Reeves

Aa
Bb
Cc
Dd
Ee

Laurent Clerc

Education: Teacher

An education is based on communication. But what if there was no standardized approach to teaching, communicating, or respecting you where you lived? And what if where you lived was the United States? Enter Laurent Clerc, the first deaf teacher of the deaf in the United States.

Trauma

Laurent was born on December 26, 1785, in a small village in France. When he was one year old, he fell into a fire. The trauma resulted in a large scar on the right side of his face and a loss of both his hearing and sense of smell. Laurent had no formal schooling until he was twelve, when he enrolled in a school for deaf students in Paris. He excelled and was asked to stay with the school as an assistant teacher, and then he took on some of the most challenging courses.

The Voyage

A young man named Thomas Gallaudet traveled to Europe to learn about deaf education and bring back teaching methods to the United States. He was frustrated by his experience until he met Laurent. Thomas studied with Laurent, learning about sign language and how the Parisian school for deaf students operated. Thomas and Laurent worked well together and became friends. When it was time for Thomas to take his learning back to the United States, Laurent was persuaded to come along. During the long voyage, Thomas learned sign language from Laurent, and Laurent learned English from Thomas.

Sign Language

The two men created their own school for the deaf in Hartford, Connecticut. Thomas was the school's principal. Laurent was busy at the school. He taught Thomas, the students, and hearing men who wanted to study deaf education. In the United States at the time, there was no standard sign language used by the deaf community. Students came to the school with signs they developed at home or within their local community. So, when Laurent taught his students, he used what he knew best: French Sign Language. His students would take this learning and blend it with their own signs. Laurent's influence was so significant that these signs became popular and ultimately became American Sign Language (ASL). Today, about two-thirds of ASL signs are linked to French Sign Language and Laurent.

Many Firsts

In 1818, when it was time to seek more funding for deaf education and their school, Laurent went to Washington, D.C., becoming the first deaf person to stand in front of Congress. The next day, he became the first deaf person to meet the president of the United States at the White House. His visits persuaded Congress to eventually pass a bill that would offer financial stability to the school. When Laurent first left France to follow Thomas, he said he would come, but only briefly. But during his time in the United States, he helped form a revolutionary school, inspired ASL, started a family, and changed how the United States viewed deaf education. Laurent passed away on July 18, 1869.

Go Give It a Try!

Have you ever tried to learn ASL? There are books, virtual resources, and probably even local classes you can attend to learn this language that is distinctly its own. ASL is not a signed representation of English; it has its own sentence structure that does not follow the rules of the spoken English language.

Booker T. Washington

Education: Teacher

Sometimes, our actions and choices can lead to greatness and growth for others. And yet, at other times, our words and decisions can be revisited with a new lens that results in controversy. That is the story of Booker T. Washington, the son of an enslaved woman, who became a teacher and a champion for industrial education.

Emancipation

Booker was born on April 5, 1856, in Hale's Ford, Virginia, to an enslaved woman who worked as a cook for a plantation owner. After emancipation (when enslaved people in the United States were given their freedom), Booker's mother moved her family to West Virginia.

EDUCATION

Hard Work

At the age of nine, Booker worked packing salt and then in a coal mine. He could go to school, but only after his work laboring with salt or coal was complete. But Booker desired even more education. When he was older, he walked five hundred miles (805 km) from his home to what is now known as Hampton University. He made the journey almost all by foot and with no money. Booker got a job as a janitor to pay for his education at the university.

A Foundation for Tuskegee

After graduation, Booker taught kids at a school during the day and adults at night. When he was twenty-five years old, he was selected to lead a new school for other African Americans. The school is now internationally known as Tuskegee University. Booker's new school, where he led and taught, had two small buildings, no equipment, and very little money. When he passed away thirty-four years later, there were one hundred well-equipped buildings, a thousand-plus students, a large faculty, and the funds to continue the work he had begun.

Communication and Controversy

Booker took pride in his ability to debate and communicate his opinions. However, his views on desegregation (the ending of laws that separated Black and white people) were controversial. While other leaders in the Black community were speaking out against segregation and focusing on the beginnings of the civil rights movement, Booker wanted African Americans to focus more on their economic advancement, which angered other Black leaders. He wanted his fellow African Americans to work toward financial security by pursuing an education that developed their industrial and farming skills instead of focusing on their rights as citizens.

Recognition and Legacy

During his lifetime, Booker wrote a dozen books. In 1901 he was the first African American to be invited to dinner at the White House by President Theodore Roosevelt. Booker died on November 14, 1915. Today, his school, Tuskegee University, continues a legacy of success. The university is now the nation's number one educator of African American aerospace engineers. Booker's legacy has been controversial. His focus on education was admirable, though others have challenged his views as offsetting the civil rights movement and limiting the advancement of Black individuals in the United States.

Go Give It a Try!

To fully understand how far Booker T. Washington walked to get an education, use digital resources to search what is located five hundred miles (805 km) from your home. What cities, sites, and possibilities are that far from you? Have you ever been to any of these locations? And now imagine walking that distance.

1
3
2
4

John Dewey

Education: Teacher

Could doing chores actually be a learning experience? That is what educational philosopher John Dewey believed. He even designed a whole school around the idea that when we complete chores, we learn new skills, including how to be a member of a community.

Early Life

John was born on October 20, 1859, in Burlington, Vermont. He attended the public schools in Burlington, where he excelled. At the young age of fifteen, John became a student at the University of Vermont. His favorite topic to study was philosophy, which is studying knowledge itself: how humans think and how things work. When John graduated four years later, he was second in his class.

Research and Teaching

John taught in Pennsylvania and then in his home state of Vermont. While teaching, he continued to study philosophy, having in-depth conversations with his former teacher. He decided to continue his education and further study philosophy at universities, later taking on the role of teacher in the philosophy department at several universities.

Think Creatively

Based on his studies, John believed that humans rely on their habits in their day-to-day lives, but when changes occur, they are forced to think creatively to regain control. He insisted that education had to change and be available to everyone. John thought that students at a young age needed to learn to break free of their normal habits and think creatively for themselves.

An Experimental School

In 1894 John and his wife Harriet started an experimental primary school in Chicago where John could test out his educational ideas. His own children attended the school. John believed that kids learned best by doing. He criticized schools for focusing too much on preparing kids for later life when they should be learning for their lives now. John understood that for real learning to occur, students had to feel involved and see how their learning was relevant to their lives.

Community

Through his work at the primary school, John believed that classrooms should be communities where students work together and help one another. He strongly encouraged students to take on chores at school, which helped them understand their ability to contribute to the greater society. Specifically, John believed that chores should not be assigned by gender—all students should learn to sew and cook, not just girls.

Legacy

John died on June 1, 1952, and left a rich legacy of educational thinking. Though John's ideas have also been misunderstood, misapplied, or completely dismissed by others as too wild and not centered on academic success, his research changed education, with his ideas adopted in countless classrooms around the globe.

Go Give It a Try!

The next time you are asked to help with chores at school or home, take a minute to think about how you are contributing to the classroom or your family. What is now possible for everyone because of your work? And what did you learn by completing your chores? Why not offer to take care of a chore before you are asked?

Dr. Alfred Mayer Neumann

Health: Social Worker

If you are narrowly escaping death because of who you are, you would probably be thinking about survival, making it through the next few days. Or would you begin to think about how you had been given a new opportunity to support so many others? This is how Dr. Alfred Mayer Neumann viewed his life after escaping the unthinkable. He had a new chance to positively impact the lives of others.

Supporting the Community

Alfred was born in 1910 in Vienna, Austria. He earned a law degree from the University of Vienna. When Hitler and the Nazis began their occupation (takeover) of Austria, Alfred worked as a counselor and organized resources for Jewish families in need. He helped get them emergency housing, set up programs for learning new trades for work, and dealt with immigration problems. He became a critical part of the Jewish community's survival.

Escape from Austria

In 1938 Alfred was scheduled to be sent to Dachau, a Nazi death camp. His mother pleaded with and ultimately bribed the officials, who gave Alfred seventy-two hours to leave the country. And like that, Alfred was running for his life, ultimately making it to the United States. In New York City, he attended school for social work. He had already been doing this work in Austria, but now he was receiving formal education on the topic.

Supporting the Displaced

As a social worker, Alfred worked in several states supporting vulnerable communities, especially those taken from their homes, an experience he knew all too well. Eventually, Alfred made it to Denver, where he served as the executive director and vice president of the Jewish Family and Children's Service of Colorado. He completely re-envisioned the family counseling program and developed new initiatives focused on adoptions and immigration services.

SHALOM

Used as a greeting, the word *shalom* means "peace." Beginning in 1954, Alfred worked with several others to create a program called SHALOM Denver that supported Holocaust survivors and later included refugees of other conflicts around the world. Reimagining his work in Vienna, Alfred's team provided housing, employment, job training, and the necessary social and emotional support their clients desperately needed.

Celebrate

On June 30, 1982, the Colorado governor proclaimed that it was Dr. Alfred M. Neumann Day. Later, Alfred was named a Social Work Pioneer by the National Association of Social Workers. Alfred passed away on March 3, 2002. This pioneer and advocate for displaced people wanted nothing more than to live a life that improved human existence, and he had done just that and more.

HEALTH

Go Give It a Try!

June 30, 1982, was Dr. Alfred M. Neumann Day. Honor someone incredible in your life with a day just for them, and no, not their birthday. Create a certificate for them, offer a special meal, and possibly even put up decorations. Celebrate all that they do for you and others. Not only will they be overwhelmed with joy but you will be, too.

John Myron Rockmore

Health: Social Worker

A pioneer is someone who has original ideas and helps open new possibilities for others. They are often leaders who inspire others to join their cause or champion their ideas. John Myron Rockmore was a pioneer in the field of social work. He envisioned and advocated (fought) for the importance of social workers in supporting those with mental illness, especially those in the military.

Diplomas and Degrees

John was born in 1913 in Brooklyn, New York. He attended college and graduated with an education degree. In 1939 John received a diploma from the New York School of Social Work, today known as the Columbia University School of Social Work. He worked for the New York Department of Social Services and the Education Bureau until World War II broke out.

Military Service

During the war, John became the chief of military psychiatric social work in the army's first-ever "mental hygiene unit." He worked as a psychiatric social worker, a special kind of social worker who supports people who have intense mental health needs. This may mean coordinating their care, providing therapy, or making sure they are hospitalized. Those serving in the military had mental health needs just like other people but had the additional impacts of the war bearing down on them.

Consulting

When World War II ended, John became a consultant to the Surgeon General of the U.S. Army. His advice became essential in expanding access to social work programs within the military and establishing policies in the new world of mental health support. John was very proud of his time in the army and was awarded a medal and Citation for Legion of Merit for his work to support mental health programs for military members. The Legion of Merit is an award in the U.S. military given to individuals for exceptional service and achievements.

Necessary Treatment

John worked as the director of social services at a treatment center in New York, taught at Columbia University, and later became the first director of social services for the Connecticut Department of Mental Health. He continued at the Department of Mental Health for twenty-three years. Over time, John helped to make social work be seen as a necessary part of mental health treatment alongside nursing and psychiatry. He advocated that social workers who focused on mental health care would also need to provide counseling and resources to family members of those being treated for mental illness, as well as the importance of aftercare. He wrote more than eighty articles on social work and mental health. John died on October 12, 2002, leaving behind a legacy of care and support for those struggling with mental health in and out of the military.

Go Give It a Try!

The U.S. Department of Veterans Affairs (VA) has hospitals around the nation supporting the physical and mental health of military veterans. Locate which VA hospital is closest to you and create a gratitude poster for the patients, complete with an image and inspirational words. Deliver the poster to the hospital for the staff to display for the patients.

Luther Christman

Health: Nurse

Leader. Trailblazer. Legend. Icon. These words were used to describe Luther Christman later in his life. But this isn't how his story began. His story, a lesson in overcoming challenges, reminds us not to give up. Sometimes you just need to change your approach.

Denied Access

Luther, the son of a coal miner, was born on February 26, 1915, in Summit Hill, Pennsylvania. He was interested in a future as a nurse. And it didn't take long for him to face resistance. He was a man trying to join a field comprised of mostly women. When World War II broke out, Luther wanted to serve his country and tried to join the Army Nurse Corps. The Corps did not allow him to join because he was a man. He later applied to two different university programs and was refused admission for the same reason. Luther was called names because of his desire to be a nurse.

A New Tactic

Though some of the challenges that Luther faced would make many people give up on their goals, it made him only more determined to be a part of a field he believed in. Instead, he tried a new strategy and worked and did research in psychology. That led to leadership roles at several university nursing programs. His desire to join nursing led him to become a leader who would change the field from the inside.

Advocacy and Inclusivity

Throughout his leadership in university settings, Luther advocated (fought) for men to be included into the nursing profession. He also believed that the field should include everyone who wanted to serve those who were most vulnerable and in need of health care. As the first male dean of the School of Nursing at Vanderbilt University, he became the first dean to hire African American women as faculty members.

Elevating the Profession

As a leader, Luther sought to elevate the profession with strong standards of excellence for all nurses. His belief was that nurses could give the best care to their patients with access to continual education and learning from practicing nurses at the university level. He wanted to provide nurses more time with their patients. His idea was to give administrative assistants the non-nursing tasks that nurses may have traditionally taken care of.

Recognition

In 1974 Luther helped institute the National Male Nurse Association, which later became the American Assembly for Men in Nursing. In 2004 he was the first man admitted into the American Nursing Association's Hall of Fame. Then, in 2007, the association established the Luther Christman Award to recognize men who significantly contributed to the nursing profession. Luther died on June 7, 2011. From his complicated beginnings trying to join nursing, Luther went on to positively influence and uplift the profession for nurses everywhere.

Go Give It a Try!

Not every nurse in your life will be named to the Nursing Hall of Fame. Take time to recognize someone you know in the nursing community for their efforts. Create a video, make a social media post, or send a message to show your appreciation for their inspiring work.

Whitney Young Jr.

Health: Social Worker

One role of a social worker is to help identify supports for people who face challenges in their lives. Whitney Young Jr. didn't just work as a social worker; he lived as an advocate for those who continually battle for access to their civil rights.

Tensions and Common Ground

Whitney was born on July 31, 1921, in Lincoln Ridge, Kentucky. Whitney always dreamed of becoming a medical doctor. But from 1942 to 1944, he served in the U.S. Army, and things went in a different direction. While in the army, Whitney was part of a construction crew of Black soldiers supervised by white officers. Tensions between the two groups of men were high. Whitney worked with the two groups to come to common ground. This interaction prompted Whitney to rethink his future goals, and after the war, he set his sights on a career in social work.

The Urban League

Whitney worked with the Urban League in several states and ultimately became the executive director of the National Urban League for ten years. The Urban League is an organization that supports African Americans and other underserved urban residents. When Whitney stepped into his role, the association was centered more on providing services and addressing middle-class issues. Whitney realized that his desire was for the organization to get involved with direct action and focus on the needs of poor people in the city. Under his leadership, the organization became a leader in the civil rights movement.

Collaboration and Action

The Urban League's active role in the American civil rights movement, under the leadership of Whitney, led to the organization's involvement in planning the March on Washington for Jobs and Freedom, where Martin Luther King Jr. delivered the now famous "I Have a Dream" speech. Whitney spoke that day, pleading with attendees to not just show up to march but to take action for their civil rights. Whitney and Martin were friends and collaborators, meeting with government leaders. Whitney himself advised and worked with several U.S. presidents on the topics of race, urban communities, and war.

Architecture

Whitney advocated for more people of color to join the architecture profession so that they could respond to their communities' needs. He spoke at national meetings of architects and challenged the inequality in housing available to people living in the city. Whitney called for architects to be more involved in social issues and use their work to respond to what communities of color required.

The Medal of Freedom

In 1969 Whitney was awarded the Medal of Freedom, the highest civilian award the United States has to offer. President Lyndon B. Johnson awarded him this honor based on his remarkable accomplishments focused on civil rights. Whitney passed away unexpectedly on March 11, 1971. This loss was felt throughout the country, and President Nixon spoke at his funeral. After his death, awards were created in his honor, his portrait was included on a postage stamp, and the university where he received his education in social work renamed the school in his name.

Go Give It a Try!

Architects are a significant part of our lives. They design houses, offices, schools, restaurants—any building you see. Use blocks, plastic bricks, or common household objects to create a city. Consider the purpose of each building and its location based on the other buildings.

Edward F. Krise

Health: Social Worker

Can you really make progress as a team if you are not open to understanding and empathizing with your teammates? This was the question at the center of Edward F. Krise's work as a social worker in the military and within the broader community.

Military Enlistment

Edward was born on June 28, 1924, in Detroit. He grew up in Washington, D.C. Edward later enrolled as a university student in Rhode Island, where he attended a single semester until he joined the U.S. Army. He served in World War II as a tank driver in North Africa, then went on to fight in Italy. During the Battle of Anzio, an attack by the Allies in Italy, Edward was taken prisoner. He spent fourteen months in a prison in Germany until he escaped.

Back to School

After World War II, Edward returned to university life and graduated with a degree in sociology. He then went on to study at the University of Chicago. While in Chicago, Edward lived at the Hull House, a settlement house that supported the local community in need and whose staff received international recognition for their work. While there, Edward participated in many community activities, learning firsthand the importance of social workers connecting with those in need, helping in crises, and building community.

Then, Back into the Military

To kick off his career in social work, Edward became the executive secretary of the North Dakota Youth Council, that is, until the Korean War broke out, calling Edward back into active duty. In 1951 he became an officer with the Army Medical Services Corps. He was one of the first social work officers in a newly established military-based social work program.

Battling Racism

As a social worker, Edward was responsible for crisis intervention and the role of relationships in supporting military effectiveness. It is with this lens that he became the first leader of the Department of Defense Race Relations Institute. Beginning in 1970, he worked to dismantle racism from within the military through education, relationships, and awareness of the history of racism in the United States. He believed that for a functioning team to be successful in military combat, service members had to be able to trust and value one another. His work included partnering Black and white soldiers throughout their time in the Institute and having teams complete community service activities together.

Recognition

Edward received significant recognition throughout his military service, including a Bronze Star, a Purple Heart, and a Silver Star for "Gallantry in Action." He was twice awarded the Legion of Merit for his work on race relations. The National Association of Social Workers presented him with the Social Work Pioneers Award for his creative work within the profession he cared so deeply about. Edward passed away on December 4, 2003.

Go Give It a Try!

Conflicts happen; they are a part of relationships. The next time you face a conflict, before reacting, start by calming your mind and body with breathing exercises, such as "elevator breathing." Breathe in, imagining you are going up the floors of a tall building. Then take another breath and slowly release it at each "floor." When you reach the "top," take one last big breath and slowly exhale, imagining you are taking the elevator back down to the lobby, feeling your whole body relax.

21
37/8 +
= X Y
a
b
c
X 5
4/2

Jaime Escalante

Education: Teacher

What is possible when you believe in others and their potential, and they believe it, too? And what about when everyone else sees them as unmotivated and without a promising future? You come alongside them and make them believe they can achieve whatever they set their sights on.

In Their Footsteps

Jaime Escalante was born on December 31, 1930, in La Paz, Bolivia, to two parents who were teachers. He followed in their footsteps, teaching math and physics in Bolivia for twelve years before deciding to move to the United States. He came to the United States with only three thousand dollars and the English words "yes" and "no" in his vocabulary. But what Jaime had was perseverance.

Perseverance

Though Jaime was a teacher in Bolivia, he couldn't get a job in the United States as a teacher without getting different degrees and learning English. To put himself through school, he mopped floors in a coffee shop and then was promoted to cook. Later he was a technician for an electrical company. All the while, Jaime was learning English and taking classes in math and physics. When he was forty-three, he took a pay cut to begin his first teaching job in the United States at Garfield High School in Los Angeles.

High Standards

Jaime had high standards for himself, as he had clearly shown his whole life, but he also had high standards for his students and those around him. But at Garfield, he was given the lowest-level math classes where it was clear no one had any hopes for his students to succeed, including the students themselves. Though Jaime felt like giving up, his new mission was to motivate those who were seen as lacking ambition. He became the ultimate performer in class, telling jokes and using props to help his students understand challenging math concepts. He even required students to answer a homework question before entering the classroom, ensuring they had done their work at home to be ready to learn together.

Advanced Placement Success

But Jaime envisioned more for his students; he designed an AP (Advanced Placement) calculus course, starting with only a handful of students each year. In 1982 eighteen of his students passed the difficult AP calculus exam, resulting in a major celebration. However, the students' scores were challenged, and Jaime and his students were accused of cheating. He again saw this as the broader community not believing in the power of his students, but he believed in them. The students retook the test, with most of the students passing the challenging test yet again.

Recognition

Educators from around the country came to his school to watch the engaging way that Jaime made math come alive for his students. He received several national awards. An award-winning movie was even produced about his efforts in the classroom. Jaime died on March 30, 2010, due to cancer. After his death, the United States Postal Service released a stamp in his honor.

Go Give It a Try!

The Postal Service often recognizes individuals for their work with a stamp designed in their honor. Who in your life would you design a stamp for? Review recent stamp designs online and create a stamp recognizing this everyday hero in your life, using paper and drawing materials or digital resources. Though you won't be able to use the stamp to send the letter, be sure to present them with their honor.

Hector Hugo Gonzalez

Health: Nurse

Sometimes, barriers prevent us from reaching our full potential or pursuing a job that would better our whole lives. Hector Hugo Gonzalez saw the obstacles for people who wanted to help others and did something about it.

Deep Roots

Hector is proud of his family's deep roots in Mexico, which date back to Spanish settlers in the mid-1700s. He remarked on his family's legacy in Mexico, saying they were there "before Mexico was Mexico, before Texas was Texas, and before the United States was the United States!" Hector himself was born on March 9, 1937, in Roma, Texas.

Education

Hector studied nursing in San Antonio in the 1960s. Male nurses were so rare then that his nursing school didn't even have a restroom for men. He went on to earn a master's degree and then entered the Army Nurse Corps. He served for two years and obtained the rank of captain. Later, while teaching, Hector pursued a PhD In 1974 he was the first Mexican American registered nurse to earn a doctorate.

Removing Barriers

When he became the chairman of the Department of Nursing Education at San Antonio College, Hector had a new vision for educating nurses. He wanted to remove all barriers holding people back from pursuing a career as a nurse. He designed a two-year nursing program that was seen as revolutionary at the time. The program was flexible and offered courses entirely at night. This decision allowed those with children or other jobs to attend school and earn their degree. Students could attend classes full-time or take it slower and go part-time. He secured the largest amount of private money for nursing scholarships ever at the college. Today, a scholarship fund in his name continues to make nursing school a possibility for male nursing students who may need financial assistance.

With Hector in this leadership position, removing barriers to education, San Antonio College had one of the highest numbers of male and minority nursing students in the country.

Celebrating Students

Not only did Hector remove barriers for students in the nursing program but he also saw value in uplifting students in all areas of education. When he devised his new plans for nursing at San Antonio College, he invited art students to design a new logo for the nursing program. The college used the winning logo, which also won several design awards.

Go Give It a Try!

Are you part of a club or group that could use a new logo? It's time you designed one! Think about what colors and images could represent the club. Look at some of your favorite logos for teams, stores, or restaurants. Use hands-on materials or a digital resource to design your logo and begin using it to gain interest in what your club has to offer.

Preston Dyer

Health: Social Worker

There are many ways to help others, and many professions provide opportunities to better the community. But our awareness of these roles is only as broad as our experience. Preston Dyer grew up wanting to help others, and against all odds and hurdles, he ended up becoming one of the most influential social workers alive.

Sermons and Church Services

Preston was born on April 28, 1938, in Atlanta. Growing up, the only person that Preston really saw helping other people was the pastor of his church. Preston loved the idea of helping others; it was what drove him. He wasn't excited about writing and preaching sermons for church services. It was helping people that inspired him. Preston applied to Baylor University in Texas to become a pastor with the support of his mom, who had been secretly saving for his college education for years.

A Change in Plans

Preston's grades weren't the best, but thanks to glowing references, he was admitted to the college on probation. This meant he didn't meet all the school's entry requirements but could be admitted and work hard to earn a permanent place there. At school, Preston met with an adviser who suggested he investigate other careers that focused on service beyond being a pastor. He landed on social work, especially supporting people with mental health needs. His parents were not happy with this decision; they had their own views of what a social worker did and what their son's life would be like. But Preston was focused on the good he could do for others, especially in mental health.

Probation

When it was time for graduate school, Preston was again admitted on probation. He worked hard and graduated with great grades and a master of social work degree. Preston spent several years working in Louisiana and Georgia until he received a call from Baylor University. Officials at the college Preston had graduated from were calling him back to develop a complete social work program. The program was outstanding. Preston had done remarkable work, but he needed a doctorate to stay in his position. He had so much self-doubt about applying to another school, questioning if he was a good-enough student. He enrolled at Texas Woman's University, again on probation. Two years later, he graduated with top honors and a doctorate in sociology. He was the first man to receive that degree from the university.

Better Together

Preston and his wife, Genie, started marriage enrichment courses. They taught their courses around the country and to diverse audiences, including individuals without homes. Their work together prompted Genie to go back to school and earn a PhD, opening the doors for the husband-and-wife team to begin teaching a course at Baylor together. Their course focused on marriage and family sociology. It was helpful for students because they were hearing and learning from both partners in a marriage. Preston taught this course for twenty years, most of it alongside his wife. In 2014 Preston was recognized as the "most influential social worker alive" by the Social Work Degree Guide.

Go Give It a Try!

Who is an adult in your life whom you see helping other people? Interview them about what drives their mission, what types of education they received, and what goals they have for the people they work with. What does their day-to-day work look like? Use your interview to spark a conversation about this remarkable person with others.

Ronald G. Lewis

Health: Social Worker
Education: Teacher

EDUCATION

HEALTH

What if your life and your interests inspired meaningful research? And what if that research went on to inform a national law that changed how generations of children were cared for and supported? Enter Ronald G. Lewis, a strong social worker, teacher, and advocate.

Unique Challenges and Joys

Ronald, a citizen of the Cherokee Nation, was born on December 3, 1941, in Muskogee, Oklahoma. As a citizen of the Cherokee Nation, Ronald grew up understanding the unique culture, challenges, and joys of being an indigenous (native) person. Striving to support people much like himself, he went to school to become a social worker. In 1974 Ronald became the first American Indian to receive a PhD in social work.

Many Firsts

Ronald was called the "Father of American Indian Social Work" and had many notable "firsts." Beyond being the first American Indian to receive a PhD in social work, he was also the first American Indian to be tenured in the University of Wisconsin system. When someone is tenured at a university, it means that they are a permanent employee and are provided certain protections. Ronald was also the first American Indian to be a full professor of social work and the first indigenous person named as a "dean" in Canada.

Teacher

Having taught at several universities, spoken around the country, and developed programs for indigenous populations, Ronald became the leading expert in American Indian social work. He researched issues that were specific to their families and communities, including the care of children and alcoholism. His research and efforts inspired many young indigenous people working at the university level.

Indian Child Welfare Act

In 1978 Ronald's research informed the creation of the Indian Child Welfare Act. This law created rules for adopting and fostering American Indian children in the United States. The law states that children born and living within an American Indian nation will continue to live within their community whenever possible. Ronald was an advocate who spoke up when he knew there was a better solution that met the needs of the American Indian people. Ronald met with members of Congress and even U.S. presidents to advocate for issues most important to him. Ronald passed away on April 14, 2019, from cancer.

Go Give It a Try!

Whose land are you on? Use an online resource to research which indigenous people originally lived where you are now living. Don't stop there: Investigate their culture further and share your learning with your family and friends.

Cliff Morrison

Health: Nurse

Even in their darkest, most painful hours, humans crave connection. This is what Cliff Morrison believed as a nurse, and because of him, the care of those diagnosed with AIDS was completely transformed.

Starting Early

Cliff grew up in Live Oaks, Florida. He didn't set out to be a nurse; he was simply looking for a way to help support his family. No one in his family had graduated from high school or attended college, and everyone had to pitch in to contribute to the family's earnings. At the age of twelve, Cliff took a job as a janitor at a local hospital. He mopped floors and took out the trash. After a year of spending time in the hospital and around patients, he asked to take care of patients. Cliff became a hospital orderly, supporting patients with day-to-day tasks and getting them from one place to another. He held this job through his high school graduation.

Change of Plans

Cliff's new plan was to attend nursing school, become the first person in his family to attend college, and then use his earnings to attend medical school to become a doctor. At the time, he had seen men only in the role of doctors and women only as nurses. But he grew to love being a nurse and went on to earn several nursing degrees, including in public health.

Human Contact

Cliff moved to San Francisco and was working in a hospital when the AIDS epidemic began. AIDS is a serious virus that prevents your body from fighting off illness and disease. At the time people were in severe pain, and many were dying. Back then, there were no medicines or treatments that could save infected people's lives. Doctors and nurses who cared for patients with AIDS did their best to avoid contact out of fear of this new illness. Cliff, who had always felt a deep need to care for others at all costs, did what seemed extraordinary at the time: He made those ill with the disease feel like humans. All the patients wanted was to be treated like people. Cliff reached out to touch and comfort them and refused to wear the space-suit-like protective gear that those around him were wearing. He felt that he knew enough about the disease to know that providing compassionate medical care wasn't going to infect him with the disease.

A New Kind of Care

Because of his efforts to connect with patients, Cliff was asked to be a consultant and help start a new section of the hospital specifically for AIDS patients. Some of the goals of this new care team were to treat the patients with dignity and respect, to allow visitors at almost any time of day, and to redefine the term *family* to allow close friends to visit patients. Touch was also important; those who were sick and dying craved physical contact. Health care facilities around the country later adopted Cliff's methods.

Go Give It a Try!

Patients in hospitals or care facilities crave connection with others. Connection doesn't have to be physical connection. You can create cards that offer encouragement or funny jokes and send them to local hospitals to be distributed by the staff to patients who would appreciate them. Work with a team, club, or your friends to create as many cards as you can.

5B

Yu "Phillip" Xu

Health: Nurse

When a nurse moves to the United States from another country, there can be challenges, misunderstandings, and frustration from both the patients and the nurse. But how can both parties learn to approach one another with empathy (understanding and sharing the feelings and experiences of others)? That is what Yu "Phillip" Xu strove to explore throughout his life's research.

Lifelong Student

Yu was born in 1961 in Zheng Zhou, China. He went to school in China, studying English and education until he moved to the United States to attend a PhD program for education. In 1996 Yu completed a degree in nursing from a community college in Alabama. And in 1999 he completed a master's degree in public health nursing. He then taught and led nursing programs at several universities. Yu's pursuit of learning took him from studying English to education to nursing, and now to educating future nurses.

Supporting International Nurses

Yu knew firsthand what it was like navigating life and work in the United States as an English language learner. Researching how to support international nurses in the United States became his life's work. He published more than fifty-six research reports and articles on the subject. Yu advocated for the professionalism of international nurses and their excellent knowledge of nursing practices. However, the English language can be challenging and lead to confusion.

Speak for Success

Yu developed a training program in Las Vegas to support international nurses called Speak for Success. In the program, Yu and a speech pathologist worked with nurses to teach them about the uniqueness of the English language and American culture. Jokes or phrases that may make sense or be funny to native English speakers led only to confusion for international nurses. Yu's successes with this program and his research led to his work as a consultant to nursing programs nationally and internationally. He stressed to the medical community that though language was a temporary barrier, the diverse lived experiences of international nurses connected to the ever-diversifying population of the United States.

Recognition

Yu served as president of the Asian American/Pacific Islander Nurses Association. He won awards for excellence in research from universities he worked with. But he saw that his real recognition came from the successful transition of international nurses into the American health system. Yu passed away on July 9, 2013, after battling cancer for years.

Go Give It a Try!

Try learning a new language. Sign up for a course offered at your school or community center. You can look for available apps or technology resources to support your learning. Consider what language you have always been interested in learning and jump in. You have to start somewhere.

WELCOME
TO Fabulous
LAS VEGAS
NEVADA

Joe Hogan

Health: Nurse

What happens when challenges stop you from achieving your goals? Do you give up? Or do you question the way things have always been done? Joe Hogan went with the second choice.

Seeking an Education

Joe earned an associate nursing degree and worked in a hospital. But he wanted more. Joe knew that additional education would make the difference and provide him with more opportunities. He began considering his options for pursuing a bachelor's degree in nursing. But when Joe, who lived in Columbus, Mississippi, researched programs he could apply to, he found that the nearest school was 150 miles (241 km) away.

Very Few Options

It appeared his only option, a co-ed program, was far from home and from the work he was already doing. However, the Mississippi University for Women (MUW) was nearby and had a bachelor's program in nursing. So, in 1979 Joe applied to the school. He was a qualified candidate, a registered nurse, and met all the requirements for admission. But Joe was denied access to the program because he was a man. The university did tell him that he could take classes at the school, but they wouldn't count for credit toward an actual degree.

Challenging the Decision

The whole reason Joe wanted to attend the school was to advance his career; to do that, he needed a degree, so Joe challenged their decision. He took MUW to court for violating his rights as an American citizen. With his first attempt, the court sided with the university. The court said that maintaining MUW's identity as a school for women was significant because it provided excellent opportunities for women. But Joe pushed on, and his case ultimately ended up at the Supreme Court.

The Supreme Court

In 1982 the Supreme Court ruled that MUW's policy was unconstitutional and that Joe and others could attend the publicly funded university. Justice Sandra Day O'Connor was the first woman appointed to the Supreme Court and had the honor of delivering the majority opinion in this case. She supported and explained the court's reasoning for calling MUW's actions unconstitutional. Joe's case ended discrimination based on gender in all publicly funded nursing schools in the entire country. Joe didn't give up when he faced a challenge to his future goals; he kept pushing and questioning and changed access to nursing programs for generations to come.

Go Give It a Try!

Is there a rule at your school that you're frustrated by? First, research why the rule was created by asking adults or older students for their perspective. You may find a good reason for the rule to exist. If not, write an opinion paper to be shared with your principal that includes other students' feedback, why you think the rule should be changed, and how you believe it should be modified. Don't forget to include how you feel this change will benefit the students and staff of the school. Present your opinion to the principal and follow up for feedback on your idea.

Mississippi Unive
for Women

Sir Jonathan Elliott Asbridge

Health: Nurse

As we grow, it is important to not forget where we have been and what we have learned. You never know when an experience will inform your future self. This was true for Sir Jonathan Elliott Asbridge, who never forgot where he started.

Resistance

Sir Jonathan, born in 1959 in Cardiff, Wales, had his first taste of nursing when he began work as a cadet with the St. John Ambulance Service in South Wales. He knew at a young age that he wanted to pursue nursing as a career, but his parents were less than excited and strongly fought back. This wasn't the future they wanted for him. Well, Sir Jonathan's story was just beginning.

Many Positions

Sir Jonathan attended nursing school and continued his schooling at a university. With so many possibilities within the nursing profession, Sir Jonathan went from being a staff nurse to a charge nurse in a critical care unit, then an inpatient manager, a general manager, and the director of Clinical Care Services. Eventually he became a director of nursing, then a chief nurse and deputy chief executive. Every step of the way, he was learning alongside other remarkable nurses and gaining firsthand knowledge of life as a nurse. With each new leadership role, Sir Jonathan kept his experience as a practicing nurse central to his decision-making process and the support of his colleagues.

Advocacy and Professionalism

Sir Jonathan was named the inaugural president of the Nursing and Midwifery Council in the United Kingdom. In this role, he took the experiences from his many nursing roles to inform his decisions that would lead to advocacy for nurses and midwives. (A midwife is someone who cares for a mother and her child during the birth of a baby.) Sir Jonathan redesigned and improved how emergency care is provided across the United Kingdom and set goals for wait times in the A&E (accident and emergency) department. He knew that for patients to receive the best care, the trainings and procedures for nurses had to improve. And nurses needed to be treated as professionals and provided with support that made them feel safe and secure in their work.

Knighthood

Since at least 1860, on the King's or Queen's birthday, individuals are awarded medals, decorations, and appointments. These recognitions celebrate the great works of citizens. On June 17, 2006, Sir Jonathan received such an honor. He was knighted for his dedication to the National Health Service and the advancement of the nursing profession. Thankfully, his family's reluctance about his career choice didn't hold him back from pursuing his dream.

Go Give It a Try!

Contemporary knighthood is an honor and has nothing to do with learning to joust, ride a horse, or shoot an arrow. But have you ever given archery a try? Research local camps or classes that teach the basics of archery. Though this new skill will probably not lead to your future knighthood, it may just become your new favorite activity.

Kurt Russell

Education: Teacher

Hope is a desire for something to happen. Hope involves trust in the future. So, when National Teacher of the Year Kurt Russell says, "I still have hope," it means something special. These four simple words reveal the truth that a situation might be complicated or frustrating, but you can still have trust in what could happen next.

The Three Wise Men

Kurt was born on October 21, 1971, in Oberlin, Ohio. As a kid, Kurt visited family in Alabama, where his parents were from. In the houses of family members, he saw paintings of Jesus, President John F. Kennedy, and Martin Luther King Jr. He had so many questions about these three men, prompting his love for learning. Kurt's questions were met with stories from his mom about her experiences with segregation (the separation of Black and white people) and the civil rights movement in Alabama.

Seen and Valued

In kindergarten, Kurt's teacher Francine Toss further ignited his passion for learning. She read the class a book about Martin Luther King Jr. that made Kurt feel seen and valued. In the eighth grade, Kurt had his first Black male teacher, Larry Thomas, who taught math. In Thomas, Kurt saw someone who looked like him in front of a class full of engaged students. Kurt saw how teachers have the power to support and motivate others. At that moment, he made a decision: He would one day be a teacher who would inspire and challenge his own students.

The Dream Job

Kurt became a history teacher in the same school he was a student in: Oberlin High School. He called it his dream job. He began teaching general history classes and then designed his own courses about African American history, Black music, and race, gender, and oppression. His goal for each class was to set a safe, inclusive environment for exploring experiences and stories while facing uncomfortable topics. Kurt wanted his students to feel seen, heard, and valued, just as Francine Toss had done for him as a kindergartener.

Coach

Beyond his classroom, Kurt became the head coach of the Oberlin Boys Varsity Basketball team. He viewed his role as an extension of the classroom. Through the relationships built on and off the court, he encouraged the boys he worked with to be resilient and confident. His players had to learn to work together while processing both success and hardship.

National Teacher of the Year

In 2022 Kurt was first named the Ohio Teacher of the Year and then selected as National Teacher of the Year. In this new role, Kurt met with teachers, leaders, families, and students across the country to advocate for opportunities for students and highlight the need for more teachers of color to join the profession. When asked about the current state of education, Kurt responded, "I still have hope." He has hope in educators across the country who provide love and normalcy when the world feels unkind. And he has hope in the inspiring students who will create a better world into the future.

Go Give It a Try!

Kurt has hope in students, teachers, and for the future of education. What is one thing you are hopeful about? Make a poster for your room or a sign for your locker with your hopeful statement. This visual will help remind you to focus forward even when you feel challenged.

Daniel Vijayaraj

Health: Nurse

A life experience can change everything. We may witness an act of kindness that inspires our own acts of selflessness many years down the road, and that was true for a young Daniel Vijayaraj.

Early Experience

Daniel is originally from the Keeladi village in India. As a child, his mom had to have a major surgery. Daniel stayed by her side in the hospital throughout her recovery. During their time in the hospital, Daniel noticed that the nurses who took care of his mom were gentle and respectful of her needs. They showed great patience with both Daniel and his mom. A child himself, he thought about how the nurses treated his mom as if she were their child in need of care and reassurance.

The Spark

While his mom continued to recover from her surgery, the nursing staff taught Daniel how to clean wounds. His mom required medicine, and the nurses taught Daniel how and when to give her the medicine she needed. This was the spark. Learning how to care for someone else when they needed it most—and in this case, someone who had cared for him so thoughtfully since he was born—prompted Daniel to pursue a nursing career.

Nursing as a Career

In 2001 Daniel started working as a nurse in England at South Tees NHS (National Health System) Trust. Over time, he continued to advance his career, learning about different nursing specialties and taking on new roles. One of those roles was to serve as a mentor to young nursing students. His mission was to offer the same care, explanations, and patience the nurses had provided him as a child when his mom was in the hospital.

Recognition

In 2022 Daniel was honored with the Nightingale Award from the South Tees NHS Trust. The award recognizes nurses who have gone the extra mile regarding patient care. Florence Nightingale, the award's namesake, was from England and the founder of modern nursing who elevated the role of nurses by focusing on patient care. Notably, Daniel's nomination came from several patients who remarked on the exceptional care they received from him. Daniel, the first nurse from India to receive this prestigious award, found the whole experience rather humbling. He viewed his recognition as a challenge to further increase his dedication to his profession and the mentorship he provides to nursing students.

Go Give It a Try!

Have you ever considered being a positive mentor for younger kids at your school or in your community? Research mentorship programs available to you or talk with a school principal about setting up a program. Consider the focus of your mentorship program and what you would like to accomplish. You could read alongside younger students, teach a specific skill, or play games with them. The key is to form a connection through communication and meet with them regularly to build a positive relationship.

Miguel Cardona

Education: Teacher

What happens when someone doesn't believe you can amount to much? Sometimes, their disbelief in you makes you more driven to do your best and redefine your potential. Miguel Cardona, a child growing up in public housing who didn't even learn English until kindergarten, never gave up. His drive has taken him to Washington, D.C., where he relentlessly advocates for students and teachers.

Puerto Rican Proud

Miguel was born on July 11, 1975, in Meriden, Connecticut. The son of two Puerto Rican parents, Miguel grew up in a public housing community, speaking Spanish as his first language. He only started learning English when he enrolled in kindergarten. His family celebrated their heritage through music. Miguel learned to play the bongo drums and played alongside his brother and dad at community events, including the town's Puerto Rican festival.

More Than Capable

When Miguel was in school, he often felt that people had lower expectations for what he could achieve. This only made him even more hungry to prove them wrong, to show everyone what he was capable of. In high school, Miguel studied at a technical school focusing on car repair while taking college preparatory classes. When it was time to apply to college, he started down a path in art education because of the influence of his incredible art teacher. But Miguel ultimately settled on elementary education. He saw the promise and the potential in their young eyes and knew he wanted to be their champion.

Classroom Experience

Miguel started his education career in a fourth-grade classroom in the same school district he attended as a child. At twenty-eight, he became the youngest principal in the state's history, leading an elementary school with exceptional programming for preschoolers, bilingual students, and students with sensory needs. In 2012 Miguel received the National Distinguished Principal Award for the state of Connecticut. After ten years in this role, he became the district's assistant superintendent.

Tour Guide

Remembering his roots and experiences as an English language learner, as assistant superintendent, Miguel would take every new hire on a tour of the district. He wanted these new educators to see the diverse communities they were serving, to give them an understanding that all of these students were now their students. He was committed to making a strong public education available for all students and took this belief to the state level as the commissioner for education in Connecticut.

U.S. Secretary of Education

On March 2, 2021, Miguel was named the twelfth U.S. Secretary of Education. In this new role, he dreamed of possibilities to positively impact the more than sixty-five million students in the United States. He wanted them to receive an excellent education that valued who they were as individual learners and with teachers who knew they were supported by a leader who was also an educator.

Go Give It a Try!

There are parts of your community you have never visited and maybe even some great surprises to discover. Make a map of your local community, including areas of interest you know about. Take the map as you walk or drive around your neighborhood with an adult, discovering new locations. Add your new sites to your map to share later with others.

EDUCATION

Babak Mashhadi Ebrahim

Education: Teacher

EDUCATION

Equity is different from equality. Equality means everyone receives the same thing, whereas equity recognizes that not all people start from the same place and need special adjustments to fix imbalances. Babak Mashhadi Ebrahim uprooted his whole life for equity and continues to work with his students, using equity as his guide.

A Life-Changing Decision

Babak immigrated to the United Kingdom from Iran in 2000. The move wasn't an easy decision, and it would change not only his life but also the lives of his family members. Babak, the father of two girls, wanted to provide his daughters with more opportunities. In the United Kingdom, his daughters could experience more opportunities than in their home country, which limited women's rights and access to education.

Access for Girls

Babak began work as a math and computer science teacher. With his focus on equity-driven teaching, Babak made a disheartening discovery. Though the United Kingdom was a place where he knew girls and women could thrive and be successful, in his classroom, girls were underrepresented. Those who were enrolled participated less than their male classmates and lacked confidence. Babak decided he needed to be the solution by offering girls an opportunity to thrive.

Cyber Girls

Babak formed his school's first Cyber Girls team. The team of girls would work together to learn about cybersecurity practices and put their learning to the test during competitions. In the United Kingdom, the National Cyber Security Centre hosts a CyberFirst competition. Babak signed up the team. In 2002 the team of girls won first place; in 2023 they reached the finals. But there was more than just the competitions. In his classes, Babak featured women speakers, offered coding competitions, and organized technology showcases. The goal was to encourage more girls to consider a future in technology.

Coaching

Babak noticed an imbalance of equal access for girls compared with boys in other areas. His daughters showed an interest in soccer, leading him to coach his school's girls' soccer team. Babak wanted to ensure that all opportunities available for his male students were accessible to his female students and, especially, his daughters. In Babak's heart, he knew that all children deserved a chance to succeed. And he was going to be part of the solution.

Pandemic and Recognition

During the COVID-19 pandemic, Babak wanted all students to have access to technological learning. He started after-school clubs, workshops, and collaborations with businesses. And, in 2023 Babak was named one of fifty finalists for the Global Teacher Prize, the winner of which receives $1 million.

Go Give It a Try!

There are downloadable cybersecurity games that are suitable for adults and students alike. With the help of an adult, locate one of these games as you develop and apply a basic understanding of defense strategies.

Peter Tabichi

Education: Teacher

Going to school is something that a lot of people take for granted. But countless kids around the world have little access to teachers, technology, and transportation to school. Peter Tabichi knows this truth all too well, but this empowering teacher will stop at nothing to provide a world-class education for his students.

Access to Education

Peter was born in 1982 in a rural part of Kenya, Africa. He grew up as one of eight kids in a family of teachers. His dad and several of his cousins were teachers. Peter's dad worked diligently to provide his children with the best education they could access, but that didn't mean it was easy. Peter had to walk more than four miles (6.5 km) every day to school. There he saw teachers' power to inspire students to reach for their potential.

Simplicity and Justice

Peter became a Franciscan friar, which is a specific role within the Catholic Church where men dedicate themselves to a life of poverty centered on simplicity, justice, and the care of others. Peter carries these values wherever he goes, especially in his classroom. He began teaching math and science in a rural school community in the Great Rift Valley in Kenya. The community is impacted by famine (extreme lack of food), drought (extreme dryness), and community conflict. Many of his students come from different tribes and villages. Peter started a peace club, where students who would have typically gotten involved in fights engaged instead in tree planting, sports, and activities that prompted them to work together and learn about one another.

Beyond the Classroom Walls

The school where Peter had been teaching had one desktop computer, no access to Wi-Fi, no kitchen, and only one teacher for every fifty-eight students. For Peter, being an educator isn't just about the walls of his classroom. He works with community members, teaching them about drought-resistant plants and the potential of renewable energy (energy that comes from a source that will not run out). Students in his classroom engaged in a project where they grew local plants to generate power. The project won the students a national award and invitations to travel around the world to share their research findings.

Good in the World

Peter hopes that students will believe in their potential. They are. In just a couple of years, with his support, the number of students attending university doubled. For Peter, his work has never been about himself. It has always been about the good he put out into the world. But people did take notice. In 2019, out of ten thousand nominations, Peter received the Global Teacher Prize, an international recognition of teachers. He was awarded $1 million, a staggering amount of money for an individual who had always given 80 percent of his teacher's salary back to his community. With his winnings, Peter hoped to bring Wi-Fi, a modern computer lab, and water to his students.

Go Give It a Try!

Research which drought-tolerant plants are native to your community. These plants can offer access to food, add beauty to your space, and provide habitats for local wildlife. Work with an adult to plan a way to start these plants in a yard or container. You will need less water to help these plants thrive.

Jermar Rountree

Education: Teacher

Oh, it's as easy as riding a bike! Have you ever heard someone say this statement to describe an activity? But what if you never learned how to ride a bike? Physical education teacher Jermar Rountree decided to change his students' lives with this very realization.

Human Connection

Jermar was born on October 6, 1984, in Waterbury, Connecticut. As a kid, Jermar was never really sure how long he would be at at any elementary school because he switched schools often. He quickly learned how to be adaptable, how to make friends, and the power of making people laugh. The strong relationships he built at each school taught him the power of human connection and how to cope with difficult challenges.

Correction Officer

In college, Jermar made a commitment with his roommate to become a correction officer, undergoing rigorous training. All the while, he felt a strong pull toward teaching. Jermar started work as a correction officer when, one day, he came upon a nineteen-year-old who was in and out of the facility. This young man had always struggled with reading and couldn't even read a letter his parents had sent him. Jermar read it to him, and it said that his parents could no longer support him based on his poor decisions. The letter was heartbreaking for the young man and confirmed what Jermar knew all along: Becoming a teacher was his calling. He wanted to help young people form a strong foundation at an early age, set them up to be successful, and help them even when others seemed to have given up on them.

The Bikes

Jermar started teaching at a school in Washington, D.C., where he taught physical education to pre-K through eighth-grade students. One day, he realized that most of his students, living in a city environment, had never learned to ride a bike. Jermar worked with community partners and bought twenty-four bikes for his students to use. Not only did he teach them about balance and road safety, but he continually did emotional and mental check-ins to see how they were feeling throughout their learning. It can be hard to learn something new, and he wanted to offer them the support they needed to be successful.

Freedom

With their new bikes, the students saw their city, Washington, D.C., like they had never seen it before. Learning how to ride a bike with Jermar had offered them new freedom to ride past the National Zoo, the White House, and national monuments. Who knows where Jermar's students will go next because of the confidence and human connection he provided them?

Recognition

That kid who had formed relationships at each new elementary school he attended was now focused on building relationships with his students and their families. And in 2023 Jermar was named the District of Columbia Teacher of the Year. He was later recognized as one of five 2023 National Teacher of the Year finalists.

Go Give It a Try!

How often do you do an emotional and mental check-in with yourself when you are learning something new? When you are learning something new, stop, take a breath, and check in with yourself. Are you proud of your work? Are you feeling energized or frustrated? Do you feel lost and confused? Once you understand where you are emotionally, consider what support you need to keep the new learning going.

Will Pooley

Health: Nurse

To fight a deadly illness is one thing. To then contract this fatal illness brings about a whole other set of challenges. Fighting your way back to health and then returning to your mission of saving others takes a brave hero. This is the story of Will Pooley.

Part of the Solution

Will was born in Suffolk, United Kingdom. In 2013 he qualified as a nurse. Africa had always been on Will's mind as a place he had wanted to work. So, in 2014 he traveled to Sierra Leone to work with a nonprofit. Will heard about how an Ebola virus outbreak was out of control, especially in one Sierra Leone hospital unit. He knew he needed to be part of the solution: the care the patients were receiving. He made up his mind and began the journey that would change everything.

Fight Against Ebola

Ebola is a rare but often fatal disease that causes high fevers and bleeding inside the body. At the Ebola treatment center where Will worked, most patients died from the horrible disease, including several of his fellow nurses. The center had difficulty getting enough staff to care for the infected patients, meaning his patients were frequently left alone in the evenings. Often, Will would come to work in the morning to find that patients he had cared for had passed away during the night. He continued to do the best he could with the resources he had, prompting him to improvise, but what they needed most were more nurses.

Infection

On a Friday, six weeks after starting at the hospital, Will woke up with a sudden fever. After testing, it was confirmed that he had contracted Ebola. To the best of his memory, Will had always worn his personal protection equipment and was incredibly careful with his patients. But one time he cared for a small baby who had tested negative after the mother had died. Later, the baby tested positive. Will's positive diagnosis prompted him to be flown out of the country and back to England in an isolation tent set up in the back of a transporter airplane.

Care

In England, Will was scared; he knew firsthand what this virus had done to people he had cared for and worked alongside. He received the best care in the world for his Ebola infection, including experimental medicine. Only after his health improved did Will begin to wrestle with his own ability to access remarkable care versus what his patients could acquire in Sierra Leone. It was this truth that sent him back to Africa, where he would continue to fight the fatal disease.

Emotional Connection

At the age of thirty, a year after his airlift out of Sierra Leone, Will began work at the very same hospital in London that saved his life after he contracted Ebola. He felt an emotional connection to the hospital and knew that in this place he could continue caring for patients, giving back what he had been given—a new chance at life.

Go Give It a Try!

Africa is a huge continent with more than fifty diverse countries. Spend some time researching this amazing continent to find out what the most commonly spoken language is. Or what is the most populous country? What other countries besides Egypt have pyramids? And what unique building material is used in Tunisia for good luck? What other unique facts can you learn about this richly diverse continent?

Ranjitsinh Disale

Education: Teacher

How does someone become a change maker? They have awareness, advocate, and find solutions to obstacles. For teacher Ranjitsinh Disale, becoming a change maker meant changing his career aspirations, learning a new language, challenging the poor treatment of girls, and providing his students with opportunities beyond their available resources.

A Change of Plans

Ranjitsinh was born on August 5, 1988, in Paritewadi, India. He grew up in Maharashtra, dreaming of becoming an IT (information technology) engineer. Decisions and plans were made that resulted in Ranjitsinh enrolling in engineering college. But it wasn't all he thought it would be, and he was left wondering, "What do I do now?" His dad suggested that he investigate becoming a teacher. Ranjitsinh resisted at first, but after only a few days in a teacher training program, he realized that teachers are the world's change makers. And he wanted to be part of that movement.

Next to the Cattle Shed

In 2009 Ranjitsinh had his first teaching position at the Zilla Parishad Primary School. The building needed repairs and was located between a cattle shed and a storeroom. Most of the girls who attended the school were from local tribal communities, where teenage marriage was common and a girl's education wasn't seen as a priority. Girls' attendance at the school would sometimes hit 2 percent. Ranjitsinh saw himself as part of the solution. He worked to fix up the school, advocated for all his students to attend, and did everything in his power to support his students' learning.

Solution Seeking

One obstacle for Ranjitsinh is that he didn't speak the primary language of his students, Kannada. The textbooks available to his students weren't even written in their language. He began learning Kannada to communicate and connect with his students and their community, and translate their readings. Ranjitsinh saw that their books were limited in their information and didn't offer his students a chance for individual learning. So, he redesigned them, adding a QR code into every book. Now, he could provide his students personalized learning opportunities with audio recordings, video lectures, and further readings they could access anywhere. This strategy was so successful that the practice was soon adopted by national organizations in India and brought to schools nationwide.

Successes

In 2016 his school was named the best school in its district. The attendance of Ranjitsinh's students rose to a point where 100 percent of the girls were attending school, and teenage marriage had become nonexistent in the village. One of his female students went on to graduate from university, an accomplishment that seemed near impossible before Ranjitsinh became their teacher. In 2016 the government of India named him the Innovative Researcher of the Year. In 2020 Ranjitsinh won the Global Teacher Prize, an award that comes with a $1 million prize. He decided to take half of this award money and split it up among the nine other finalists. He believed that with these funds, these nine educators could further their incredible work for students and ultimately change the world.

Go Give It a Try!

Is a friend's or a relative's birthday coming up? Record a video of yourself offering a birthday greeting. Use a QR code generator, available for free online, to create a QR code that links to your video message. Combine the virtual and the physical by printing the code and adding it to a card you send in the mail.

Adrian Bermudez

Health: Nurse

Look around at the adults in your life. Are they your role models? Do they set a standard for you to follow? This was true for Adrian Bermudez, who saw in his family members the challenges and triumphs of caring for others. He saw possibilities for himself and now supports others to do the same.

Family Inspiration

Adrian was born in 1997 in New York City. He grew up in East Brunswick, New Jersey, with inspiring nurses in his life. His mom was an intensive care unit (ICU) nurse in New York, and his grandma was a nursing director at a nursing home in New Jersey.

Baseball Injury

When Adrian was ten years old, he suffered a dramatic baseball injury. He had a torn shoulder labrum, an injury that is like the kind that Major League Baseball players can get. He was the youngest patient the surgeon had ever seen with this injury. Adrian had to spend lots of time in the hospital during and after the surgery with many doctors and nurses. Spending so much time in the hospital at an early age sparked his interest in the medical field.

Men in Nursing Club

Adrian went on to study nursing at the University of Pittsburgh. While there, Adrian cofounded the university's first Men in Nursing Club. The club would become a place for male nursing students to connect, find mentorship, and recruit others to join nursing. Mentorship, when someone with lots of experience provides guidance and support to someone with less experience, is really important to Adrian. Throughout nursing school, he had the mentorship of his family and the upperclassmen who had been through the program. He knew he wanted to pay it forward by making mentorship a priority of the new Men in Nursing Club.

Hands-on Learning

Exciting others about the nursing field, especially other young men, is important to Adrian and inspired him to take their club on the road. He and some of the club's members started visiting local Pittsburgh high schools to answer questions about what being a nurse is like. After the discussion, the students were then able to participate in hands-on learning about nursing skills. Students could meet with college admission counselors about what it would take to get involved in a nursing program. Adrian's goal of exciting others about nursing was coming true.

COVID-19

COVID-19 changed life for everyone, but especially for those in health care. Adrian worked alongside his mom in the same New York City ICU during the COVID-19 pandemic: two nurses, mother and son, working to care for vulnerable patients at the same hospital where Adrian was born. For Adrian, it has always been about connecting with patients when they may be experiencing the worst days of their life.

Go Give It a Try!

Check out clubs that are available for you to join at your school or within your local community based on your interests. You could find a new group of like-minded people. If you are looking for a club that doesn't exist, it is time to start one. Think about the purpose of your club, what you would accomplish together, and what adult support may be needed to make it all possible.

About the Authors

Jonathan Juravich began teaching elementary art outside of Columbus, Ohio, in 2005. Still actively teaching art to young students, his personal and professional focus is on the importance of social and emotional learning in our daily lives. This is his favorite topic for research and discussion, including his PhD dissertation, his TED Talk "How Do We Teach Empathy," his limited-series podcast *The Art of SEL*, and his Emmy award-winning digital drawing program "Drawing with Mr. J." In 2018, Jonathan was named Ohio Teacher of the Year and one of four finalists for National Teacher of the Year. In 2023, he was named the National Elementary Art Teacher of the Year by the National Art Education Association. He lives in Columbus, Ohio, with his family.

Richard V. Reeves is the founding president of the American Institute for Boys and Men (AIBM) and the author of *Of Boys and Men: Why the Modern Male Is Struggling, Why It Matters, and What to Do about It*. Before founding AIBM in 2023, Richard was a senior fellow at the Brookings Institution. While at Brookings, he focused on policies related to economic inequality, racial justice, social mobility, and boys and men. He is also a regular contributor to the *New York Times*, the *Atlantic*, *National Affairs*, and other publications.

Between 2010 and 2012, Richard was director of strategy to the United Kingdom's Deputy Prime Minister. A former European Business Speaker of the Year, his other previous roles include director of Demos, the London-based political think tank, principal policy advisor to the Minister for Welfare Reform, research fellow at the Institute for Public Policy Research, and journalist for the *Guardian* and *Observer* newspapers. He earned a BA from Oxford University and a PhD from Warwick University. Richard tweets from @richardvreeves and his website is richardvreeves.com.

About the Illustrator

Chris King is an illustrator and artist from West Yorkshire, in the north of England, whose illustrations have an impactful style based on strong line work and a lifelong love for comic books. His figurative illustrations have led him to work for leading media outlets, publishing houses and consumer brands worldwide. When not drawing Chris can be found making music and walking the many moorland trails near his home.

Acknowledgments

This project would not have been possible without Richard Reeves' research and H.E.A.L. concept that challenges us to rethink stereotypes and possibilities. May this book serve as an inspirational resource to introduce our children to male role models in the fields of health, education, arts, and literacy who have made this world a more empathetic and beautiful place. To the men who are featured in this book, thank you for your work and for stepping into spaces with confidence, curiosity, and creativity. Thank you for sharing rich, vulnerable stories of your lived experiences. I am certain that your profiles will inspire future leaders and dreamers.

Thank you to Jonathan Simcosky and the Quarry Books team for their guidance throughout this process, and their dedication to this project. Endless gratitude to Chris King who breathed life into these profiles with his beautifully expressive portraits. And to my family, thank you for your unwavering support throughout all the seasons of our life together.

—Jonathan Juravich

Also Available

ISBN: 978-1-57715-673-4

ISBN: 978-1-57715-675-8

ISBN: 978-1-57715-672-7